Marx Joyce
Hardy Machiavelli Montaigne Chesterton Cooper Emerson Austen
Defoe Abbott Melville Haggard Hugo
Carroll Christie Eliot Grimm
Stoker Molière
Wilde Maupassant Byron
Engels Schiller
Garnett Einstein Fitzgerald Smith
Goethe Hawthorne Kafka
Cotton Dostoyevsky Hall
Baum Kipling Doyle Willis
Leslie Dumas Henry Nietzsche
Flaubert Turgenev Balzac
Stockton Vatsyayana Crane
Burroughs
Curtis Tocqueville Whitman Gogol Verne
Homer Widger Tolstoy Vinci
Darwin Thoreau Busch
Potter Freud Zola Twain Plato Scott
Lawrence
Kant Jowett Stevenson Dickens
Andersen Cervantes Burton Hesse Harte
London Descartes
Poe Aristotle Wells Voltaire
Hale James Hastings Cooke
Bunner Shakespeare
Richter Chekhov Chambers Irving
Doré da Swift Dante Shaw Wodehouse Benedict Alcott
Pushkin
Newton

California, 1849-1913, or, the rambling sketches and experiences of sixty-four years' residence in that state

L. H. (Lell Hawley) Woolley

Imprint

This book is part of TREDITION CLASSICS

Author: L. H. (Lell Hawley) Woolley
Cover design: Buchgut, Berlin – Germany

Publisher: tredition GmbH, Hamburg - Germany
ISBN: 978-3-8424-5647-1

www.tredition.com
www.tredition.de

California

1849-1913

or

The Rambling Sketches and Experiences of Sixty-four Years' Residence in that State

By

L. H. Woolley

Member of the Society of California Pioneers
and of the Vigilance Committee of 1856

California

1849-1913

Trip Across the Plains.

The year 1849 has a peculiarly thrilling sensation to the California Pioneer, not realized by those who came at a later date. My purpose in recording some of my recollections of early days is not for publication nor aggrandizement, but that it may be deposited in the archives of my descendants, that I was one of those adventurers who left the Green Mountains of Vermont to cross the plains to California, the El Dorado—the Land of Gold.

In starting out I went to Boston, New York, Philadelphia, Cincinnati, St. Louis and Independence, Missouri. Here I joined the first mule train of Turner, Allen & Co.'s Pioneer Line. It consisted of forty wagons, one hundred and fifty mules, and about one hundred and fifty passengers. We left the frontier on the fourteenth of May 1849, and here is where our hardships commenced. Many of us had never known what it was to "camp out" and do our own cooking. Some of the mules were wild and unbroken, sometimes inside the traces, sometimes outside; sometimes down, sometimes up; sometimes one end forward and sometimes the other; but after a week or two they got sobered down so as to do very well.

Our first campfire at night was on the Little Blue River, a few miles from Independence, it was after dark when we came to a halt, and it was my friend Gross' turn to cook, while the rest brought him wood and water and made a fire for him by the side of a large stump. I knew he was a fractious man, so I climbed into one of the wagons where I could see how he got along. The first thing that attracted my attention was the coffee pot upside down, next away went the bacon out of the pan into the fire. By this time he was getting warm inside as well as outside, and I could hear some small "cuss words"; next he looked into the Dutch oven, and saw that his dough had turned to charcoal. I got down into the wagon out of sight, and peeked through a crack; he grew furious, danced around the fire, and the air was full of big words. Finally we got a little coffee and some cakes and bacon, then I undertook to do a little sleeping but it was no go. Thus ended my first night on the Plains.

In the morning we started on our journey to travel over a level untimbered, uninhabited country for nearly four hundred miles, without anything of especial interest occurring save cholera, from which there was terrible suffering. We lost about seventy-five of our number before we reached Fort Laramie, seven hundred miles from Missouri.

There was a Dutchman in my mess by the name of Lamalfa, who understood but little of English. We had dubbed him "Macaroni" for having brought a lot of the stuff with him and on our second night out it came his turn to stand guard. He was detailed to the inner guard and instructed as to his duties. On the relief of the outer sentinel and his return to camp, Lamalfa issued the challenge which was to repeat three times "Who comes there?" and in case of no response to fire, and as the outer sentinel came upon him he called out "Who comes there three times" and fired; fortunately he was a poor shot and no harm was done.

It seems that "Macaroni" was not aware of there being an outer guard.

When near Fort Childs, four hundred miles out, all the passengers left the wagons, except the drivers, and walked on in advance, leaving the wagons light (they were canvas covered). There came up one of those terrible hailstorms, common in that country, which pelted the mules with such severity as to cause them to take fright and run away, breaking loose from the wagons which were taken by the storm in another direction, first wheels up, then top, until the latter was all in rags; then they stopped. When we came into camp at night they looked sorry enough and you would have thought they had just come out of a fierce fight.

We pursued our journey along the south bank of the Platte until we reached Fort Laramie, capturing some antelopes and occasionally a buffalo. Up to this time we had had a great deal of sickness in camp. I remember one poor fellow (his name I have forgotten), we called him Chihuahua Bob; he was a jovial, good natured fellow and drove one of the eight-mule baggage wagons. I enquired about him one morning and was told that he had died during the night of cholera, and had been left in his shallow grave.

We met some returning emigrants that morning who had become discouraged and were going back to their old homes This made me think of home and friends, the domestic happy fireside, and all that

I had left behind, "but," said I to myself, "this won't do, I am too far out now; pluck is the word and I'm not going back on it."

Early next morning we were once more upon our long journey, slowly traveling towards the far, far West.

The first place of interest that presented itself to our view was a narrow passage for the river between two perpendicular rocky banks, which were about one hundred feet high and looked as though a man could jump from one to the other at the top. This was called the "Devil's Gate." Above and below was the broad prairie.

At intervals along the Platte were villages of prairie dogs, who were about the size of large grey squirrels, but more chunky' of a brownish hue, with a head somewhat resembling a bulldog. They are sometimes eaten by the Indians and mountaineers. Their earth houses are all about two feet deep; are made in the form of a cone; are entered by a hole in the top, which descends vertically some two or more feet and then takes an oblique course, and connects with others in every direction. These towns or villages sometimes cover several hundred acres and it is very dangerous riding over them on horseback.

We will now pass to another interesting object called "Chimney Rock" which is not altogether unlike Bunker Hill Monument. It stands by itself on the surrounding level country, with a conical base of about one hundred and fifty feet in diameter and seventy-five feet high where the nearly square part of the column commences, which is about fifty feet on each of the four sides. It is of sandstone and certainly a very singular natural formation. Altogether it is about two hundred feet high. I will mention here that the banks of the Platte are low, that the bed is of quicksand, that the river is very shallow and that it is never clear. One of our company attempted to ford it on foot. When about two-thirds over, in water up to his waist, he halted, being in doubt as to whether he should proceed or return. While hesitating between two opinions his feet had worked down into the quicksand and became so imbedded that he could not extricate them. Realizing his perilous position he at once gave the Masonic Grand hailing sign of distress and in a moment there were several men in the water on their way to his relief. They reached him in time and brought him safely into camp.

About this time there was considerable dissatisfaction manifested in camp on account of the slow progress we were making. Some left the train and went on by themselves, others realized the necessity of holding to together to the last in order to protect themselves as well as to care for those among us who were sick. The peculiar characteristics of the party at this time seemed to be recklessness and indifference to the situation, but the better judgment finally prevailed and we went on in harmony.

The next three hundred miles were devoid of any especial interest. This brings us to the summit of the Rocky Mountains (at South Pass) which divides the rivers of the Atlantic and Pacific Oceans, and ends their course thousands of miles apart. Here are the ever snow-capped peaks of the Wind River Mountains looming up on the north. They are conical in form and their base is about one thousand feet above the plain that extends south. This brings us to the nineteenth day of July, 1849. On the night of this day water froze to the thickness of one-fourth of an inch in our buckets. The following day we commenced descending the western slope, which was very rapid and rough. The twenty-first brought us to Green River which was swollen and appeared to be a great barrier. Here, for the first time, we brought our pontoons into use and swam the mules, so that after two days of hard work we were all safely landed on the west bank. We are now at the base of the Rocky Mountains on the west, passing from one small valley to another, until we reached a bend in the Bear River. Here let us pause for a moment and study the wonders of nature.

First, the ground all around is covered with sulphur; here, a spring of cold soda water; there, a spring of hot soda water; fourth, an oblong hole about four by six inches in the rocky bank, from which spouts hot soda water, like the spouting of a whale. It is called "Steamboat Spring." It recedes and spouts about once in two minutes. All of these are within a hundred steps of each other.

Now, our canteens, and every available vessel is to be filled with water, for use in crossing forty-five miles of lava bed, where there is neither water nor grass to be found and must be accomplished by traveling day and night. This was called "Subletts' Cutoff," leaving

Salt Lake to the south of us, and brings us to the base of the mountains at the source of the Humboldt River.

On the west side, in crossing over, we encountered a place in a gorge of the mountain called "Slippery Ford," now called the "Devil's Half-Acre." It was a smooth inclined surface of the rock and it was impossible for the mules to keep their footing. We had great difficulty in getting over it.

Now we are at the headwaters of the Humboldt River, along which we traveled for three hundred miles, over an alkali and sandy soil until we came to a place where it disappeared. This was called the "Sink of the Humboldt." This valley is twenty miles wide by about three hundred long. During this part of our journey there was nothing of interest to note. The water of this river is strongly impregnated with alkali.

About forty miles in a southerly direction from the sink of the Humboldt (now called the Lake) is old "Ragtown" on the banks of the Carson River, not far from Fort Churchill. In traveling from one river to the other there was no water for man or beast. When we were about half way we found a well that was as salt as the ocean. We reached this well sometime in the night of the first day and our mules were completely fagged out, so we left the wagons, turned the mules loose, and drove them through to the Carson, arriving there on the night of the second day. Here was good grass and fine water, and bathing was appreciated to its fullest extent.

We remained for several days to let our animals recruit, as well as ourselves, then we went back and got the wagons. We traveled westward through Carson Valley until we entered the Six Mile Canon, the roughest piece of road that we found between Missouri and California. There were great boulders from the size of a barrel to that of a stage coach, promiscuously piled in the bed of this tributary to the Carson, and over which we were obliged to haul our wagons. It took us two days to make the six miles.

Arrival In California.

Now we see Silver Lake, at the base of the Sierra Nevadas on the east side; our advance to the summit was not as difficult as we anticipated. Having arrived at this point we are at the source of the south fork of the American River and at the summit of the Sierra Nevadas. We now commenced the descent on a tributary of this river.

After a day or two of travel we arrived at a place called Weaverville, on the tenth day of September, 1849. This place consisted of one log cabin with numerous tents on either side. Here was my first mining, but being weary and worn out, I was unable to wield the pick and shovel, and so I left in a few days for Sacramento where I undertook to make a little money by painting, but it was a failure, both as to workmanship and as to financial gain. However, by this time I had gained some strength and left for Beal's Bar at the junction of the north and south forks of the American River. Here I mined through the winter with some success.

In the spring of 1850 thirty of us formed a company for the purpose of turning the south fork through a canal into the north fork, thereby draining about a thousand yards of the river bed. Just as we had completed the dam and turned the water into the canal, the river rose and away went our dam and our summer's work with it.

Winter coming on now nothing could be done until spring, so I left for San Francisco where I had heard of the death of a friend at Burns' old diggings on the Merced River, about seventy-five miles from Stockton, and knowing that his life was insured in favor of his wife I went there and secured the necessary proof of his death so that his widow got the insurance. There was considerable hardship in this little trip of about one week. On my return, and when within about thirty miles of Stockton, I camped for the night at Knight's Ferry, picketed my pony out, obtained the privilege of spreading my blankets on the ground in a tent and was soon in a sound sleep, out of which I was awakened at about two o'clock in the morning by feeling things considerably damp around me (for it had been raining). I put out my hand and found I was lying in about three inches of water. I was not long getting out of it, rolled up my blankets, saddled my pony and left for Stockton. Here I arrived at about nine o'clock, sold the pony, and was ready to leave at four o'clock for San Francisco. While waiting here (Stockton) I became acquainted with a Kentucky hunter who told me the story of his experiences of the day previous. He said:

"I came to the place where you stayed last night, yesterday morning, and was told that there were a number of bears in the neighborhood, and that no one dared to hunt them. I remarked that that was my business, and I would take a hand at it; I strapped on my revolvers and knife, shouldered my Kentucky rifle and started out. I had not gone more than half a mile, when I discovered one of the animals I was in search of, and away my bullet sped striking him in the hip. I made for a tree and he made for me! I won the race by stopping on the topmost branch, while he howled at the base; while reloading my rifle I heard an answer to his wailing for me or for his companion—it didn't matter which. Very soon a second cry came from another direction, and still one more from the third point of the compass. By this time one had reached the tree and I fired killing him. Hastily reloading, I was just in time to fire as the second one responded to the first one's howl; he fell dead; then the third arrived and shared the same fate. Having allowed the first one to live as a decoy, his turn came last; then I descended and looked over my work—four full-grown bears lay dead at my feet."

To corroborate this statement I will say that I saw one of them on the hooks in front of a butcher shop in Stockton, and the other three went to San Francisco on the same boat that I did. I met the hunter on the street about a week later and he told me that he realized seven hundred dollars for his bears. I do not make the statement as a bear story, but as a bare fact.

Life In the Mines.

The preceding pages were written about twenty years ago, and only covered about one and one-half years after leaving the Green Mountains of old Vermont. Since which time, I have experienced nearly all of the vicissitudes of the State to the present time (1913). I will now attempt to give an account of my stewardship from that time on. I date my arrival in the State, Weaverville, about three miles below Hangtown (now Placerville), September 10th, 1849. This was where I did my first mining, which was not, much of a success, on account of my weak condition caused by my having the so-called "land scurvy," brought on from a want of vegetable food, and I left for Sacramento City where I remained for a week or two and then left and went to Grass Valley. There I made a little money, and went to Sacramento City and bought two wagon loads of goods, went back to Grass Valley and started a hotel, ran it a few weeks, and the first thing I knew I was "busted."

It is now in the winter of '49 and '50 and I went to Sacramento again, and from Sacramento to Beal's Bar on the North Fork of the American River at the junction of the North and South Forks. By this time I had gained my strength so that I was more like myself, and I bought a rocker, pick, shovel and pan and went into the gulches for gold. I had fairly good luck until spring. By this time I had laid by a few hundred dollars, and I joined a company of thirty to turn the South Fork of the American River into the North Fork, by so doing we expected to drain about one-fourth of a mile of the bed of the South Fork. The banks of the river were rich and everything went to show that the bed of the river was very rich, and we went to work with great hopes of a big harvest of gold. The first thing we did was to build a dam, and dig a canal, which we accomplished in about four months. About this time snow and rain came on in the mountains, raised the water in the river and washed away part of our dam. It was now too late to build again that season.

Now you see the hopes and disappointments of the miner. While we were at work on the canal we had occasion to blast some boulders that were in our way. We had a blacksmith to sharpen the picks and drills who had a portable forge on the point of land between the two rivers. When we were ready to blast the rock we gave him timely warning, he paid no heed, the blast went off, and a portion of a boulder weighing about 500 pounds went directly for his forge and within about six inches of his legs and went on over into the North Fork. The man turned about and hollered to the boys in the canal "I surrender."

About this time the river had risen to such an extent that it was thought advisable to suspend operations until the next spring. This was a dividing of the roads, and each member had to look out for himself. I went to Mokelumne Hill, staked out some claims and went to work to sink a shaft through the lava to bedrock. The lava on the surface is very hard, but grows softer as you go down. While I was thus banging away with my pick and not making much headway, there came along a Mr. Ferguson from San Francisco, on a mule. He stopped and looked at me a minute and then said, "Young man, how deep do you expect to go before you reach bedrock?" I said, "About 65 or 75 feet." "Well," said he, "by –– you have got more pluck than any man I ever saw." He went on and so did I, and I have not seen him since. It took me about two weeks to get so that I could not throw the dirt to the surface, then I had to make a windlass, get a tub and rope, and hire a man to help me at eight dollars a day, and 50 cents a point for sharpening picks. These things completed and in operation, I was able to make two or three feet per day, and we finally reached the bedrock at a depth of 97 feet. The last two feet in the bottom of the shaft I saved for washing, and had to haul it about one mile to water. I washed it out and realized 3 1/2 ounces of very coarse gold. Now we were on the bedrock and the next thing to do was to start three drifts in as many directions. This called for two more men to work the drifts, and a man with his team to haul the dirt to the water, while I stood at the windless and watched both ends. This went on for one week. When I washed out my dirt, paid off my help and other expenses, I had two dollars and a half for myself.

About this time I was feeling a little blue and I gave directions for each man in the drifts to start drifts to the left at the end of each drift. This was done, and we went on for another week as before, and this time I came out about one hundred dollars ahead. About this time a couple of miners came along and offered me thirteen hundred dollars for my claim, and I sold it, took the dust and went to Sacramento and sent it to my father in Vermont. That paid up for all the money that I had borrowed, and made things quite easy at home.

Now, I am mining again with cradle, pick, shovel and pan in gulches, on the flats, in the river and on the banks, with miner's luck, up and down, most of the time down. However, "pluck" was always the watchword with me. I floated some of the time in water, some of the time in the air, some of the time on dry land, it did not make much difference with me at that time where I was. I was at home wherever night overtook me. But finally I got tired of that and began to look about and think of home and "the girl I left behind me."

Home Again. Married. Return to California.

In the spring of '52 I left San Francisco on the steamer "Independence" via the "Nicaragua route" for New York, arrived there in course of a month, and took train for Boston, where I found my father from Vermont with a carload of horses. This was clover for me. We remained there a week or ten days, then left for home. The "girl I left behind" was a Vermont lady but was visiting a sister in Cincinnati, Ohio. In the spring of 1853 I went on to Ohio to see the "girl I left behind me," and married the "girl I had left behind me." We then went to Vermont, where we remained until the year of 1854. In the summer of this year I had the second attack of the "California fever." I called in Dr. Hichman and he diagnosed my case, and pronounced it fatal, and said there was no medicine known to science that would help me, that I must go, so I took the "girl I left behind me" and started for San Francisco.

Vigilance Committee of 1865.

On my return to San Francisco it did not take me long to discover that the city was wide open to all sorts of crime from murder, to petty theft. In a very short time I became interested in the Pacific Iron Works, and paid very little attention to what else was going on around me until the spring of '56. Here was a poise of the scales, corruption and murder on one side, with honesty and good government on the other. Which shall be the balance of power, the first or the last?

On May 14th, 1856, James King, editor of the "Evening Bulletin," was shot by Jas. P. Casey on the corner of Washington and Montgomery streets. He lingered along for a few days and died. This was too much for the people and proved the entering wedge for a second vigilance committee. During the first 36 hours after the shooting there were 2,600 names enrolled on the committee's books. Of that number, I am proud to say, I was the 96th member, and the membership increased until it amounted to over 7,000.

Shooting of Gen. Richardson.

I will first relate a crime that had happened the November previous (November 17, 1855), in which Charles Cora had shot and killed General William H. Richardson, United States Marshal for the Northern District of California. These men had a quarrel on the evening of November 17th, 1855, between 6 and 7 o'clock, which resulted in the death of General Richardson by being shot dead on the spot in front of Fox & O'Connor's store on Clay street, between Montgomery and Leidesdorff streets, by Cora. Shortly after this Cora was arrested and placed in custody of the City Marshal. There was talk of lynching, but no resort was had to violence. Mr. Samuel Brannan delivered an exciting speech, and resolutions were declared to have the law enforced in this trial. General Richardson was a brave and honorable man, and beloved by all. He was about 33 years of age, a native of Washington, D. C., and married. Cora was confined in the County jail. We will now leave this case in the mind of the reader and take it up later on.

Shooting of James King, of William.

On May 14th, 1856, the city was thrown into a great excitement by an attempt to assassinate James King, of William, editor of the "Evening Bulletin," by James P. Casey, editor of the "Sunday Times." Both Casey and King indulged in editorials of a nature that caused much personal enmity, and in one of the issues of the "Bulletin" King reproduced articles from the New York papers showing Casey up as having once been sentenced to Sing Sing. Casey took offense at the articles, and about 5 o'clock in the afternoon, at the corner of Montgomery and Washington streets, intercepted King who was on his way home, drew a revolver, saying, "Draw and defend yourself," and shot him through the left breast near the armpit. Mr. King exclaimed, "I am shot," and reeling, was caught up and carried to the Pacific Express office on the corner Casey was quickly locked up in the station house[1].

Immediately following the shooting large crowds filled the streets in the neighborhood anxious to hang to the nearest lamp post the perpetrator of the crime. Casey was immediately removed to the County jail for safer keeping. Here crowds again congregated, demanding the turning over to them of Casey and threatening violence if denied. Mayor Van Ness and others addressed them in efforts to let the law take its course but the crowd which had been swelled into a seething mass, remonstrated, citing the shooting of Marshal Richardson, and demanding Cora, his assassin, that he, too, might be hanged.

Military aid was called to the defense of the jail and its prisoners and after a while the multitude dispersed, leaving all quiet.

Casey and Cora Turned Over to Vigilance Committee.

Sunday, May 18th, a deputation of the Committee was delegated to call at the door of the jail and request the Sheriff to deliver up the prisoner, Casey. Upon arriving at the door three raps were made. Sheriff Scannell appeared. The delegation desired him to handcuff the prisoner and deliver him at the door. Without hesitation, the Sheriff repaired to the cell of Casey and informed him of the request of the Vigilantes. The Sheriff, after going through some preliminaries, brought the prisoner to the front door of the jail and delivered him into the hands of the Committee. My company was stationed directly across the street lined up on the sidewalk. Immediately in front of us was a small brass cannon, which a detachment had shortly before secured from the store of Macondray & Co. It was the field piece of the First California Guard. It was loaded, and alongside was the lighted match, and all was in readiness should any resistance be offered. Other companies were stationed so as to command the entire surroundings. We marched from the general headquarters of the Committee at 41 Sacramento street (Fort Gunnybags), one block from the water front, up that street to Montgomery, thence to Pacific and along Kearny to the jail, which was situated on the north side of Broadway, between Kearny and Dupont streets. Other companies came via Stockton and Dupont streets[2].

Casey was then ironed and escorted to a coach in waiting and, at his request, Mr. North took a seat beside him; Wm. T. Coleman and Miers F. Truett also riding in the same conveyance. Another conference was held with the Sheriff, requesting the prisoner, Charles Cora, who had murdered General Richardson, to be turned over to the Committee. Scannell declined and asked time to consider. The Committee gave the Sheriff one hour in which to decide. In less than half that time the Sheriff appeared at the door of the jail and turned Cora over to the Committee. The Committee reached the rooms on Sacramento street about 2 o'clock. Casey was placed under guard in a room above headquarters. Cora was also removed to the Committee's rooms in the same manner as Casey, the Committee having to go back to the jail for the second time. About three hundred men remained on guard at the Committee rooms after their removal there.

Fort Gunnybags.

Our headquarters and committee rooms were at the wholesale liquor house of Truett & Jones, No. 41 Sacramento street, about a block from the water front, and embraced the block bounded by Sacramento, California, Front and Davis streets, and covered by brick buildings two stories high. The name "Fort Gunnybags" was ascribed to it on account of the gunnybags filled with sand which we piled up in a wall some six feet through and about ten feet high. This barricade was about twenty feet from the building. Guards were stationed at the passageways through it as well as at the stairs and Committee by the members of the Monumental Fire Engine Company No. 6, stationed on the west side of Brenham Place, opposite the "Plaza." Our small field pieces and arms were kept on the ground floor, and the cells, executive chamber and other departments were on the second floor.

May 19th found Mr. King still suffering from his wound, but no great alarm was felt as to his condition.

Death of James King, of William.

May 20th Mr. King's condition took a turn for the worse, and at 12 o'clock he was sinking rapidly, being weakened from the probing and dressing of the wound. He passed away. Sorrow and grief were shown by all. He left a widow and six children. He was born in Georgetown, D. C., and was only 34 years old.

Trial of Casey and Cora.

Casey and Cora were held for trial May 20th, having been supplied with attorneys and given every opportunity to plead their cases. The Committee sat all night and took no recess until the next morning when the trials were ended. The verdict of "guilty of murder" was found in each case and they were ordered to be executed Friday, May 23rd, at 12 o'clock noon. While the trial was going on Mr. King passed away[3].

Hanging of Casey and Cora.

The Committee, for fear that an attempt might be made to rescue Casey and Cora, arranged their companies, which numbered three thousand men and two field pieces, cleared the streets in the immediate vicinity and had had constructed a platform from out of the two front windows. These platforms were hinged, the outer ends being held up by cords which were fastened to a projecting beam of the roof, to which a rope had been adjusted for the purpose of hanging.

Arabella Ryan or Belle Cora was united in marriage to Charles Cora just before the execution.

About one o'clock both Casey and Cora, who had their arms tied behind them, were brought to the platform and with firm steps stepped out upon them. Casey addressed a few remarks, declaring that he was no murderer, and weakened at the thought of his dear old mother. He almost fainted as the noose was placed around his neck. Cora, to the contrary, said nothing, and stood unmoved while Casey was talking, and apparently unconcerned. The signal was given at twenty minutes past one o'clock and the cord cut, letting the bodies drop six feet. They hung for fifty-five minutes and were cut down and turned over to the Coroner. We, the rank and file of the Vigilance Committee, were immediately afterwards drawn up in a line on Sacramento street, reviewed and dismissed after stacking our arms in the Committee room, taking up our pursuits again as private citizens[4].

Yankee Sullivan.

James (or Yankee) Sullivan, whose real name was Francis Murray, had been taken by the Vigilance Committee and was then (May 20th, 1856), in confinement in the rooms of the Committee. He was very pugilistic and had taken an active part in ballot-box frauds in the several elections just previous. He had been promised leniency by the Committee and assured a safe exit from the country, but he was fearful of being murdered by the others to be exiled at the same time. He experienced a horrible dream, going through the formality and execution of hanging. He called for a glass of water, which was given him by the guard, who at the same time endeavored to cheer him up, and when breakfast was taken him at 8 o'clock that morning he was found dead in his bed, he having made an incision with a common table knife in his left arm near the elbow, cutting to the bone and severing two large arteries[5].

"Law and Order" Party.

On the 2nd of June, 1856, Governor J. Neely Johnson having declared the city of San Francisco to be in a state of insurrection, issued orders to Wm. T. Sherman to enroll as militia, companies of 150 men of the highest standard and to have them report to him, Sherman, for duty. The response was light and the order looked upon as a joke and little or no stock taken in it. So on the 7th Sherman tendered his resignation as Major General, claiming that no plan of action could be determined upon between himself and the Governor. The action taken by the Governor in this move was by virtue of the constitution of the State, his duty to enforce the execution of the laws, he claiming that the Vigilance Committee had no right to arm and act without respect to the State laws.

Terry and Hopkins Affair.

On the 2nd of June, 1856, the city was in great excitement at an attempt by David S. Terry to stab Sterling A. Hopkins, a member of the Committee. Terry was one of the judges of the Supreme Court. Hopkins and a posse were arresting one Rube Maloney when set upon by Terry. Hopkins was taken to Engine House No. 12 where Dr. R. Beverley Cole examined and cared for his wound which was four inches deep and caused considerable hemorrhage. The blade struck Hopkins near the collar bone and severed parts of the left carotid artery and penetrated the gullet. Terry and Maloney at once fled to the armory of the "Law and Order Party" on the corner of Jackson and Dupont streets. The alarm was at once sounded on the bell at Fort Gunnybags and in less than fifteen minutes armed details were dispatched to and surrounded the headquarters of the "Law and Order Party" where Terry had taken refuge, and in less than half an hour had complete control of the situation, and by 4:15 o'clock in the afternoon Terry and Maloney and the others found there had been taken to the Committee rooms as well as the arms (a stand of 300, muskets) and ammunition. About 150 "Law and Order" men together with about 250 muskets were also taken from the California Exchange. Several other places were raided and stripped of their stands of arms.

Terry was held by the Vigilance Committee until August 7th and charged with attempt to murder. Mr. Hopkins recovered and Terry, after a fair and impartial trial, was discharged from custody, though many were dissatisfied at his dismissal and claimed that he should have been held. Terry was requested to resign and resigned his position as judge of the Supreme Court.

Duel Between Terry and Broderick.

In 1859 Judge Terry had an altercation with United States Senator Daniel C. Broderick which caused the former to challenge the latter to a duel. This duel which was with pistols was fought September 13, 1859, near Lake Merced, near the present site of the Ocean House. It resulted in Broderick's death, whose last words were, "They killed me because I was opposed to a corrupt administration, and the extension of slavery." Terry was indicted for his duel with Broderick, as it came in conflict with the State laws. The case was transferred to another county, Marin, and there dismissed. During the Civil War Terry joined the Confederate forces, attained the rank of Brigadier-General, and was wounded at the Battle of Chickamauga. At the close of the conflict he repaired to California and in 1869 located at Stockton and resumed the practice of the legal profession. Some years later he became advocate for a lady who was one of the principals in a noted divorce suit. Subsequently she became his wife. Legal contention arising from the first marriage caused her to appear before the Circuit Court held in Oakland, over which Stephen J. Field, Associate justice of the United States Supreme Court, presided.

Terry and Field, Shooting of Terry.

In open court the justice proceeded to read the decision. As he continued, the tenor was manifestly unfavorable to Mrs. Terry. She suddenly arose and interrupted the reading by violently upbraiding Field. He ordered her removal from the judicial chamber. She resisted, and Terry coming to his wife's assistance, drew a knife and assaulted the bailiffs. He was disarmed, and together with his wife, overpowered and secured. The court of three judges sentenced Mrs. Terry to one month, and her husband to six months imprisonment, which they served in full. Justice Field returned to Washington, and the next year in fulfillment of his official requirements came again to California. He had been informed that Terry uttered threats of violence against his person, and therefore he was accompanied by a man employed by the Government to act in the capacity of bodyguard. On the journey from Los Angeles to San Francisco, Field and his companion, with other passengers, left the train to lunch at Lathrop. Terry and his wife, who had boarded the cars en route, also left the cars and shortly afterwards entered the same restaurant. A few minutes later Terry arose from his seat, walked directly back of Field and slapped or struck the venerable justice on the face, while he was seated. Nagle, the guard who attended Field, leaped to his feet and shot Terry twice. Terry fell and died instantly. This event occurred on the 15th day of August, 1889, not quite thirty years from the time he shot Broderick.

Hetherington and Randall.

On the evening of July 24, 1856, the Vigilance Committee had another case on their hands which called for immediate action.

Joseph Hetherington, a well-known desperate character with a previous record, picked a quarrel with Dr. Randal in the lobby of the Nicholas Hotel. They both drew their revolvers and shot: after the second report the doctor dropped and Hetherington, stooping, shot again, striking the prostrate form in the head, rendering the victim almost unconscious. He died the next morning.

The shooting was brought about through Randal's inability to repay money borrowed from Hetherington on a mortgage on real estate.

Hetherington, who was captured by the police, had been turned over to the Committee by whom he was tried, the Committee going into session immediately after the shooting, found him guilty of murder and sentenced him to be hanged.

We were again called out on the 29th and were stationed so as to command the situation. This time a gallows was erected on Davis street, between Sacramento and Commercial.

Another man, Philander Brace by name, was also to be hanged at the same time, and at about 5:30 in the afternoon of July 29th they were both conveyed in carriages, strongly guarded, to the execution grounds. Hetherington had previously proclaimed his innocence, claiming that the Doctor had shot first and he had simply shot in self-defense, but his previous record was bad, he having killed a

Doctor Baldwin in 1853 and had run a gambling joint on Long Wharf, and eye witnesses claimed that he not only provoked but shot first.

Brace was of a different nature, he was a hardened criminal of a low type. The charge against him being the killing of Captain J. B. West about a year previous, out in the Mission, and of murdering his accomplice. He had also confessed to numerous other crimes.

Hanging of Hetherington and Brace.

Thousands of people were on the house-tops and in windows and on every available spot from which a view of the gallows was to be had. The prisoners mounted the scaffold, being accompanied by three Vigilance Committee officers who acted as executioners and a Rev. Mr. Thomas. After the noose had been adjusted, Hetherington addressed the crowd, claiming to be innocent, and ready to meet his Maker. Brace, every once in a while, interrupted him, using terrible and vulgar language. The caps were adjusted, the ropes cut and the two dropped into eternity. They were left hanging 40 minutes, after which the bodies were removed by the Committee to their rooms and afterwards turned over to the Coroner. They were both young men—Hetherington 35, a native of England, had been in California since 1850, while Brace was but 21, a native of Onandaigua County, N. Y.

Ballot Box Stuffing.

The ballot boxes that had been used by Casey and his ilk were of a peculiar construction, having false slides on the sides and bottoms that could be slipped out and thereby letting enough spurious votes drop into the box to insure the election of their man or men. It was claimed that nearly the entire set of municipal officers then holding office had secured their election through this man. They were afterwards requested by the Vigilance Committee to resign their offices, but at the first election that was held on November 4th, they were all displaced by men selected by a new party (the People's party) that was the outcome of the efforts of the Vigilance Committee.

Billy Mulligan.

William Mulligan was shipped out of the State on the steamer "Golden Age" on June 5th, 1856, with instructions never to return under penalty of death. However, after three or four years of absence he returned to San Francisco. He was often seen on the street, but was not molested until sometime in the summer of 1862 when he got a crowd of boys around him on the crossing of Prospect Place and Clay street, between Powell and Mason streets. It was not long before he had trouble with them and shot into the crowd, injuring a boy, however, not seriously. The police were soon on the ground, but Mulligan had made his way into the old St. Francis Hotel on the corner of Clay and Dupont streets which was vacant at that time. The police came and they were directed to the building where Billy could be found. When the police entered they found they were half a story below the floor of a very large room in the second story. Billy was called upon to surrender. He told them that the first one that put his head above the floor would be a dead man, and knowing the desperate character they were dealing with, they thought best to retire and get instruction from the City Attorney, who told them they had a right to take him dead or alive, whereupon they proceeded to arm themselves with rifles and stationed themselves on the second floor of a building on the opposite side of the street from the St. Francis on Dupont street, and when Mulligan was passing one of the windows the police fired. Mulligan dropped to the floor, dead as a door nail. He was turned over to the Coroner and has not been seen on the streets since. Charles P. Duane is another one of twenty-seven men who were shipped out of the State and returned. He shot a man named Ross on Merchant street, near Kearny. I do not remember whether the man lived or died, or what became of Duane.

Black List.

From the book entitled "San Francisco Vigilance Committee of '56," by F. W. Smith, I quote the following, with some corrections and alterations:

"I am informed by an ex-Vigilante that the Committee roll call of '56, just before its disbandment, numbered between eight and nine thousand.

In concluding our history of this society, we will give the names and penalties inflicted on those who came under its eye during the latter year; whose conduct was so irreparably bad that it could not be excused.

Those who suffered the death penalty did so in expiation for lives they had taken. The names of these culprits are familiar to the reader. We also give the names of those who were required to leave the State; all of whom, in the archives of the Vigilantes, fall under the head of the black list:"

James P. Casey, executed May 22nd, 1856.
Charles Cora, executed May 22nd, 1856.
Joseph Hetherington, executed July 29th, 1856.
Philander Brace, executed July 29th, 1856.
Yankee Sullivan (Francis Murray), suicided May 31st, 1856.
Chas. P. Duane, shipped on "Golden Age," June 5th, 1856.
William Mulligan, shipped on "Golden Age," June 5th, 1856.
Woolley Kearney, shipped on "Golden Age," June 5th, 1856.
Bill Carr, sent to Sandwich Islands, June 5th, 1856, bark "Yankee."
Martin Gallagher, sent to Sandwich Island, June 5th, 1856, bark "Yankee."
Edward Bulger, sent to Sandwich Islands, June 5th, 1856, bark "Yankee."
Peter Wightman, ran away about June 1st, 1856.
Ned McGowan, ran away about June 1st, 1856.
John Crow, left on "Sonora," June 20th, 1856.
Bill Lewis, shipped on "Sierra Nevada,"—June 20th, 1856.
Terrence Kelley, shipped on "Sierra Nevada," June 20, 1856.

John Lowler, shipped on "Sierra Nevada," June 20th, 1856.
William Hamilton, shipped on "Sierra Nevada," June 20th, 1856.
James Cusick, ordered to leave but refused to go, and fled into the
interior.
James Hennessey, ordered to leave, but fled to the interior.
T. B. Cunningham, shipped July 5th, 1856, on "John L. Stephens."
Alex. H. Purple, shipped July 5th, 1856, on "John L. Stephens."
Torn Mulloy, shipped July 5th, 18,56, on "John L. Stephens."
Lewis Mahoney, shipped July 5, 1856, on "John L. Stephen,."
J. R. Maloney, shipped July 5th, 1856, on "John L. Stephens."
Dan'l Aldrich, shipped July 5th, 1856, on "John L. Stephens."
James White, Shipped July 21st, 1856, on "Golden Age."
James Burke, alias "Activity," shipped July 21st, 1856, on "Golden Age."
Wm. F. McLean, shipped July 21st, 1856, on "Golden Age."
Abraham Kraft, shipped July 21st, 1856, on "Golden Age."
John Stephens, shipped September 5, 1856, on "Golden Age."
James Thompson, alias "Liverpool Jack," shipped September 5, 1856, on
"Golden Age."

Many others either left of their own volition or under orders to leave the state.

Bulger and Gallagher who had been shipped out of the country on June 5th returned to San Francisco. In their haste the Committee had failed to read their sentences to them and they were not aware of the penalty of returning. They were again shipped out of the country and ordered not to return under penalty of death.

There were 489 persons killed during the first 10 months of 1856. Six of these were hanged by the Sheriff, and forty-six by the mobs, and the balance were killed by various means by the lawless element.

"Fort Gunnybags" 1903.

On March 21, 1903, the California Historic Landmarks League placed a bronze tablet on the face of the building at 215 Sacramento street that had formerly been the headquarters of the Vigilance Committee of 1856, inscribed as follows: "Fort Gunnybags was situated on this spot, headquarters of the Vigilance Committee in the year 1856." Many of the old Committee and Pioneers participated in the ceremonies. The old Monumental bell which had been used those stirring days was also in evidence and pealed out its last "call to arms."

Closing Chapter of Vigilance Committee.

As a closing chapter to the history of the Vigilance Committee of 1856, or at least the immediate cause of its coming into existence, there was sold at public auction in San Francisco on the evening of January 14th, 1913, the very papers that James King, of William, had had transcribed from the records in New York and published in his paper the "Evening Bulletin" showing the record of Casey's indictment, imprisonment and pardon, the publication of which he, Casey, resented by shooting King. In addition to these documents were sold many of the books, papers, etc., of as well as other books and papers relating to the Vigilance Committee that had been collected together by Mr. C. J. King, a son of James King of William.

Vigilance Committee Work In 1849, '50 and '51.

While there has been a great deal said about the Vigilance Committee in California in 1856, there has not been much said about it in '49, '50 and '51. That the reader may know what was going on up to that time, I must now draw largely from previously published accounts for my information, for a condensed statement.

On the 30th day of January, 1847, Mr. Washington A. Bartlet became the first Alcalde of San Francisco, under the American flag. At this time the population numbered 500, including Indians. During '47 and '48 it increased to two thousand, and by the last of July,

1849, it was over five thousand. The condition of the town at this time was terribly demoralized, gambling, drunkenness and fights on every corner. About this this came a class of offscourings of other countries and the curses to California. It was during this dreadful state of uncertainty that the famous Vigilance Committee of 1851 was organized, and it now became known that there was an organized committee for the purpose of dealing with criminals. It was about this time the case of John Jenkins came up and he was arrested and tried by the Committee, and condemned to be hanged. He was then hanged until he was dead. The tragic fate of Jenkins, and the determination manifested to deal severely with the villains had the effect of frightening many away. The steamers to Stockton and Sacramento were crowded with the flying rascals. The Sydney Coves and the more desperate characters remained. At this, time the city served notices on all persons known to be vicious characters to leave the city at once, on fear of being forcibly expelled to the places whence they had come. This was rigidly enforced and had a very wholesome effect.

The next one to come before the Committee was James Stuart, who was transported from England to Australia for forgery. It is not worth while to go into details on account of this man, for he confessed to crimes enough to hang him a dozen times. On the morning of July 11th, 1851, the taps on the bell of the Monumental Engine House summoned the entire Vigilance Committee. The prisoner was then allowed two hours grace, during which time the Rev. Dr. Mills was closeted with him in communion. After the expiration of the two hours, the condemned was led forth under a strong guard. He was taken down Battery street to the end of the Market street wharf, where everything had been previously arranged for the execution. Very soon after the procession reached the spot the fatal rope was adjusted and the condemned hoisted up by a derrick.

The hanging of Stuart seems to have been a very bungling piece of work, but this man's life was given to evil doing, and the great number of crimes confessed and committed by him would seem to say that he was not deserving of any more sympathy than which he got. This was a sorry spectacle, a human being dying like a dog, but necessity, which dared not trust itself to feelings of compassion, commanded the deed, and unprofitable sentiment sunk abashed.

Two more criminals and I am done with rough characters—Samuel Whittaker and Robert McKenzie, who had been arrested and duly and fairly tried by the Committee. They confessed their guilt and were condemned to be hanged. Their names being familiar and repulsive to all decent citizens. They were hanged side by side in public view on August 24th, 1851. The sight striking terror to the hearts of other evildoers, who were impressed by these examples that they could no longer be safe in San Francisco, such as had been suspected and notified by the Committee, quickly left the city; they, however, found no shelter in the interior.

This brings me to where I took up the Vigilance Committee of 1856.

San Francisco In 1847.

In view of the great and growing importance of the town of San Francisco (Yerba Buena), situated on the great bay of the same name, we will give our readers a few pertinent and fully reliable statements.

"The townsite, as recently surveyed, embraces an extent of one and one-half square miles. It is regularly laid out, being intersected by streets from 60 to 80 feet in width. The squares are divided into lots of from 16 1/2 varas (the Spanish yard of 33 1/3 inches) front and 50 deep, to 100 varas square. The smaller and more valuable of these lots are those situated between high and low water mark. Part of these lots were sold in January last at auction, and brought from \$50 to \$600. The established prices of 50 and 100 vara lots are \$12 and \$25.

San Francisco, last August, contained 459 souls, of whom 375 were whites, four-fifths of these being under 40 years of age. Some idea of the composition of the white population may be gathered from the following statement as to the nationality of the larger portion: English, 22; German, 27; Irish, 14; Scotch, 14: born in the United States, 228; Californians, 89.

Previously to the first of April, 1847, there had been erected in the town 79 buildings, nearly all of which had been erected within the two years preceding, whereas in the next four months 78 more had been constructed.

There can be no better evidence of the advantages and capabilities for improvement of the place than this single fact."—St. Louis "Reville," February 12, 1848.

John A. Sutter.

I remember standing on the bank of the Sacramento River, talking with Captain Sutter, in the fall of '49; he remarked, "I have moored my boats in the tops of those cottonwood trees, where the driftwood showed not less than 25 feet from the ground."

"The Plaza."

Portsmouth Square or the "Plaza," as we then called it, was located in the hub of the old settlement on the cove, and occupied half a block to the west of Kearny street, between Clay and Washington. It was the scene of all public meetings and demonstrations. It was named after the old sloop-of-war "Portsmouth," whose commanding officer, Captain Montgomery, landed with a command of 70 sailors and marines on July 8, 1846, raised the American flag here and proclaimed the occupancy of Northern California by the United States. A salute of twenty-one guns was fired from the "Portsmouth" simultaneously.

On the east side of Kearny street, opposite the Plaza, was the "El Dorado," a famous gambling saloon, adjoining which was the Parker House, afterwards the Jenny Lind Theatre, while on the north side of Washington street stood the Bella Union Theatre, and on the west on Brenham Place was the old Monumental Fire Engine House whose fire bell played so prominent a part in the days of the Vigilantes.

In the spring of 1850 the writer was in San Francisco, and made the acquaintance of Captains Egery and Hinkley, who were the owners of the Pacific Foundry. They being in need of some molding sand for small work, I consented to go to San Jose and get some for them. I engaged Mr. Watts, who had a little schooner that would carry about six tons. He was captain and I was super-cargo, and we made the trip down in about one day. I found what I wanted on the banks of a slough, loaded the schooner and returned to San Francisco. While in San Jose I came across two young ladies. I had a very pleasant chat with them. I learned later on that they were the daughters of Mr. Burnett, who became the first Governor of California. I heard no more of them until 1910, when I was on my way to Monterey to attend the unveiling of the Sloat Monument. I enquired for them of a man in the depot, and he told me that one of them was lying over there, dead (pointing in the direction), I could not help expressing my sorrow.

The captain landed me and my cargo in San Francisco in good shape, without any mishap on the voyage. I delivered the cargo in good order and was well paid.

Early Realty Values.

In 1850 I was in San Francisco and by chance was on Clay street where the city was selling 50-vara water lots in the neighborhood of Sansome, Battery and Front streets, at auction, $25 for inside lot, and $30 for corner lots. I stood there with my hands in my pockets, and gold dust and gold coin on my person that was a burden to me and bought not a single lot. There were many others who were in the same fix that I was. You may say, "What a lot of fools," and I would say, "Yes." Here is another little joke: Sometime before this I made a deposit of a sack of gold dust with Adams & Co.'s Express in San Francisco. When the time came for me to leave the city, I went into the office to draw my sack of dust. The clerk brought it forward at once and I said, "How much for the deposit?" He said, "Five dollars." Then I said, "You will have to take it out of the sack as I have no coin." He said, "Are you going to sell it?" "Yes," I said. "Well," said he, "You can sell it at the counter on the other side, and pay that clerk." "All right," said I, and sold my dust. It amounted to $425. He counted out the $25 in small change, and slipped it out onto the counter. I let it lay there until he had counted out the rest.

A Deal In "Slugs."

At this time the $50 slugs were in circulation. He counted out the $400 in a pile and took hold of the bottom one and set the pile over to my side of the counter, as much as to say, "There is your money." I said to him "There is five dollars coming to you for the deposit of the dust." He picked the five dollars out of the change on the counter. I picked up the balance of the change and put it into my pocket. I also picked up the pile of slugs by the bottom one in the same way that he handed them to me and dropped them into an outside pocket of my coat without counting them, and started for the four o'clock boat for Stockton. On my way to the wharf I thought that pile of slugs looked large and I took them out and counted them. I found that I had twelve instead of eight. I turned around and went back to the office, to the same counter and clerk, and said to him, "Do you rectify mistakes here?" He said, "Not after a man leaves the office." I said, "All right," and left the office and made the Stockton boat all right. But there were no insane asylums there at that time.

Harry Meiggs.

In the early fifties Honest Harry Meiggs (as he was called) was one of our most enterprising, generous and far-seeing citizens. His first venture was in the banking business. It was while engaged in this pursuit that he gained the name "Honest Harry Meiggs." His banking business was good for a year or so and then he conceived the idea of building a wharf at North Beach. It commenced at Francisco street between Powell and Mason streets. It extended north several hundred feet and was used for a landing place for lumber in the rough, to be conveyed to his mill on the South side of Francisco street near Powell. In order to accommodate the demands of trade an "L" was extended eastward from the end of his wharf. About this time he got into financial troubles. In October, 1854, he departed with his family for Chili between two days and passed out through the Golden Gate, and no more was heard of him for a long time. It finally became known that he was in Peru, engaged in building bridges for that government. He took contracts and was very successful and became well off in a few years. He sent an agent to San Francisco to hunt up all his creditors and pay them, dollar for dollar with interest. I knew a widow in San Francisco in the late '60s by the name of Rogers who was a creditor, who married a man by the name of Allen; I think that was in 1867. They went to Peru and saw Mr. Meiggs. He paid all she demanded, about $300. Allen returned and reported to the children that their mother died while in Peru of fever, but they never got a cent of the money.

Mr. Meiggs was born in New York in 1811 and died in Peru in 1877.

San Francisco's First Town Clock.

The first public clock ever erected in San Francisco was placed on the frontage of the upper story of a four-story building at Nos. 425-427 Montgomery street, that was being built by Alexander Austin. This was in 1852. The clock was ordered by him and brought via the "Panama Route" from New York, arriving in San Francisco on the steamer Panama.

Mr. Austin occupied the ground floor as a retail dry goods establishment and it was one of the first, if not the first, of any prominence in the city. He afterwards moved to the southeast corner of Sutter and Montgomery streets and continued there until 1869 when he was elected city and county tax collector.

The clock remained on the building until January 20th, 1886, when the then owner of the building, Mr. D. F. Walker, had it removed so as to arrange for the remodeling of the interior.

Mr. W. H. Wharff, the architect in charge of the remodeling, purchased the clock and retained it in his possession until November 24, 1911, when he presented it to the Memorial Museum of the Golden Gate Park, where the curator, Mr. G. H. Barron, placed it in the "Pioneer Room." It is to be seen there now.

Admission Day Flag.

Here is an interesting fact that has never been given publicity before, and I simply relate it as told me by Sarah Connell, the daughter of the man that carried it.

"Mr. D. S. Haskell, manager of the express and banking business of Adams & Co., conceiving the patriotic idea of having an American flag carried in the division of which his firm was to be a part, endeavored to procure an American flag, but found that nothing but flags of the size for ships or poles were to be had. He then started to find material from which to have one made, but in this he was unsuccessful also. So, undaunted, he at last found a dressmaker who lived somewhere in the neighborhood of Washington and Dupont streets, who found in her 'piece-bag' that she had brought from New York, enough pieces of silk and satin (they were not all alike) to make a flag three feet by two feet. He was so delighted with her handiwork that he gave her a $50 slug for her work[6].

"Thus it was that Adams & Co. were able to parade under the stars and stripes in that memorable parade of October 28, 1850, in celebration of the admission of California as a state into the union. After the parade Mr. Haskell presented the flag to their chief messenger, my father, Mr. Thomas Connell, and it has been in our possession since."

Mr. Thomas Connell.

Mr. Connell was one of the few of the early comers who never went to the mines, though of course, that was his intention. He started, but somewhere on the Contra Costa side—it was all Contra Costa then—he fell ill of malaria fever. There was no one with time to bother with a sick man and he was unable to proceed or return so he expected to end his life there. When the disease abated he concluded that he had no desire to penetrate further into the wilderness, so he turned his face towards San Francisco again. He was a shipwright by trade and though there was nothing doing in his line, he saw the possibilities of a boating business when there were no wharves, piers or other accommodations for freight or passengers.

One of the curious uses to which his boats were put was the carrying of a water supply. They were chartered by a company and fitted with copper tanks which were filled from springs near Sausalito. On this side of the bay the water was transferred to wagons like those now used for street sprinkling and the precious fluid was supplied to householders at a remunerative rate of twenty-five cents a pail, every family having one or two hogsheads fitted with a spigot to hold the supply.

Mr. Connell also carried the first presidential message received in the State, rowing up the Sacramento River day and night in his own boat to deliver the document at the capitol, and for sake of the sentiment he also carried the last one received by steamer as far as Oakland, whence the delivery was completed by train.

Uncle Phil Roach, Happy Valley.

Uncle Phil Roach, editor and founder of the "San Francisco Examiner," lived on Clementina street near First. He was one of those good natured, genial old men that everybody liked, was at one time president of the Society of California Pioneers (1860-1), and later elected to the State Legislature. He afterwards acted as administrator of the Blythe estate, but died before its final settlement.

The place where he lived was called Happy Valley and the only entrance to it was at the intersection of Market, Bush and First streets, this crossing being at the east end of a sand dune about 30 feet high, extending westerly about half a mile. At this time the waters of the bay came up to the corner of Market and First streets, but it was not long before this, and many other sand dunes, disappeared, being scraped and carted off to fill the nearby mud flats.

There was at this time a little wharf 50 feet wide extending out into the cove from the foot of Clay street at Davis 1550 feet to a depth of 35 feet. It was called "Long Wharf." To the north of this wharf the water lapped what is now Sansome street for a block (to Washington street) and followed the shore line to the corner of Jackson and Montgomery streets.

Early Water Supply.

My mind drifts back to the days when our water system was dependent in part upon a well near the corner of Market and First streets. This was in 1855 when the population of San Francisco was between 40,000 and 50,000. I was then living on Third street near Mission and got my supply of water from a man named Somers who conveyed water about the city to his various customers in a cart. I took water from him for about three years at the rate of $1.50 per week.

Many's the time I have gone out to the Mission hunting rabbits. All that part of the city was as wild as it ever was, sand dunes and low grounds. About three years later a company built a plank toll road on Mission street from some point near the water front to the Mission, a distance of about three miles. This made an opening through the sand dunes and that section filled up rapidly.

Postoffice.

The postoffice was situated on the lot at the northwest corner of Washington and Battery streets. It was built in 1855. Previous to the erection of this building the pioneers obtained their mail from the postoffice on Clay street and Waverly Place, and on Clay street near Kearny opposite the Plaza (Portsmouth Square), and afterwards on Clay and Kearny streets. The great fire of 1852 destroyed these places. To avoid confusion and facilitate the delivery of the mail on the day the steamer arrived, long lines were formed of people who expected letters from home.

It was a frequent occurrence to see the same people standing in place all day waiting their turn, the delivery windows being arranged alphabetically. Oft-times persons would sell their places for as much as ten and even twenty dollars.

John Parrott.

John Parrott, the banker, was a good natured man and could take a joke with much grace. Here is one: "A broker came to him one day and said: 'Mr. Parrott, I want to borrow one thousand dollars on a lot of hams in the warehouse.' 'All right,' said Mr. Parrott. It went on for some time and Mr. Parrott looked around for his ham man, but could not find him, but he found the hams and the greater part of the weight of them was maggots. Mr. Parrot was very much disgusted. Time went on for a number of years and another man came to him to borrow money on hams in the warehouse. Mr. Parrott said to him, shaking his finger before the man's face, 'No more hams, no more hams,' and walked off." It was a standing joke on the street for a long time. This was late in the '50's.

In 1858-59 I built two very good houses on the south side of Howard street near Fourth. I lived in one of them about two years and then bought on the north side of Taylor street between Clay and Washington streets and resided there 17 years.

Pony Express.

I was present when the first messenger mounted his pony to start on the first trip across the continent. He started from Kearny street between Clay and Washington, opposite the "Plaza"—this was on the 3rd of April, 1860. It was a semi-weekly service, each rider to carry 15 pounds of letters—rate $5 per half ounce. Stations were erected about 25 miles apart and each rider was expected to span three stations, going at the rate of eight miles per hour. The first messenger to reach San Francisco from the East arrived April 14, 1860, and was enthusiastically received. Time for letters from New York was reduced to 13 days, the actual time taking from 10 1/2 to 12 days. The best horses and the bravest of men were necessary to make these relays, over the mountains, through the snow and across the plains through the Indian-infested country. The distance from San Francisco to St. Joseph, Mo., was 1996 miles and the service was established by Majors, Russell & Co., of Leavenworth, Kansas.

Now I will go back a few years and pick up a little experience that was scattered along the road. In 1861 I took my family around the bay for an outing in a private carriage. We went through San Mateo, Redwood City, Santa Clara, San Jose, Hot Springs, Hayward, San Leandro, Oakland and back to San Francisco by boat. We enjoyed the trip very much without any mishap to mar its pleasure.

A Venture In Flour.

About this time I bought out Loring & Mason who were in the retail grocery business on the corner of Taylor and Clay streets. This was another venture in which I had never had any experience, "But," said I, "Here goes for what there's in it." A few days later there came a man in his buggy from over the hill with whom I was very little acquainted. He had charge of the Empire warehouse in the lower part of the city. His name was Mr. Garthwait. He called at my store and said, "Woolley, I have a lot of Oregon Standard flour in the warehouse. The storage is paid for one month, and I will sell you what you want for $6 and three bits a barrel, and you can take it out from time to time as you like." After looking the situation over for a few minutes I came to the conclusion that I could not buy any lower. I said, "Well, I will take one hundred barrels." "All right," said he, and drove off. In a few days I went down and paid for it. About the middle of December 1861 it commenced to rain in the valleys and a few days later it rained in the mountains throughout the State, and the snow commenced to melt and that, together with the rain in the valleys, started the rivers to rising, and as the rivers went up so did the flour. The water gauge at Sacramento indicated feet and inches in going up while flour indicated dollars and cents in going up. On the first of January, 1862, it was still raining and the water coming down in a greater volume. Communication was cut off from all parts of the country except by water. The Legislature was in session that winter and was obliged to adjourn and go to San Francisco to finish its labors. In order that my readers may adequately realize the greatness of this flood it is no more than fair to say that the river boats from San Francisco went up J and K streets in Sacramento City and took people out of the second-story windows. Now, then we will call this high-water mark and flour $10 a barrel and going up. During this time I was letting my customers have what they wanted at the quotation price. It continued to advance about one dollar per day until it reached sixteen dollars per barrel. At this time I had very little left and it all went at that price. Very soon after this flour came in from Oregon and the price went down, as well as the water, and the market assumed a lower level and business went on as usual. It must be remembered that all transportation at this time was either by water or highway.

A Venture In Oil.

In this year was the beginning of the Civil War and for the benefit of those who came into active life later on I will give them a little of my experience in a small way. At the time I purchased the store of which I have spoken I took over a standing contract they had with a firm in Boston to send them a specified amount of coal oil around Cape Horn, as near six weeks as any vessel would be leaving for San Francisco. I took what was on the way at that time and the shipments were continued to me. At this time it took from sixty to seventy days to get answers to letters from the East. Time and business go on. We had on an average of about two steamers a month from New York with the mails. In 1862 the war tax and stamp act came in force. It was high and quite a hardship for some but everybody paid it cheerfully and with a good grace, and felt that they were getting off easy. About this time greenbacks came into circulation as money. It was legal tender and you could not refuse it. It made a great deal of hard feeling on many occasions but after a long time it set settled down to a premium on gold, which fluctuated from day to day. Finally the premium on gold was so high that currency was only fifty cents on a dollar, that is, one dollar in gold would buy two dollars in currency. On account of this many debtors would buy currency and pay their creditors with it. This was considered very crooked on the part of the debtor. I myself was a victim to some extent. The "Evening Bulletin" exposed a great many men by publishing their names but by so doing it made enemies and it did not last long. All bills rendered from this time on were made payable in United States gold coin. My coal oil cost me fifty cents per gallon in Boston, payable in currency. The freight was also payable in currency. Now my readers will readily see that my coal oil cost me a little over twenty-five cents per gallon laid down in San Francisco. About 1863 there was an unusual demand for coal oil and it was scarce and there was very little on the way around Cape Horn, consequently the market price went up very rapidly until it reached $1.50 and $1.75 per gallon. The result was that I sold all I had in the warehouse and on the way around the Horn. I kept what I had in the store for my retail trade. I do not look upon these speculations as any foresight of mine, but the change of circumstances and conditions of the market.

Flood of '61 and '62.

The great flood of '61 and '62 was an occasion seldom known in the State. Early in December '61 it commenced to rain in the valleys and snow in the mountains. In about two weeks it turned to rain in the mountains and valleys. The melting of the snow caused the rivers to rise very rapidly, the levees gave way and the waters flooded the city. The merchants commenced to put their goods on benches and counters, anywhere to keep them above water. Families who had an upper story to their house moved into it. The water continued to rise until it reached a point so that the boats running between Sacramento and San Francisco went up J and K streets and took people out of the second story of their houses. The islands were all flooded and there was great suffering along the river besides the great loss of property. This flood did more damage than any high water since '49, but it was as an ill wind as far as it concerned my business, as I related previously.

Civil War Times In S. F.

In 1861 Dr. Wm. A. Scott, pastor of the Calvary Presbyterian church, on the north side of Bush street between Montgomery and Sansome streets, closed his services praying for the presidents of the Union and of the Confederate States. As soon as the benediction was pronounced Mrs. Thomas H. Selby smuggled him out of the side door into her carriage and off to her home, fearing the congregation, which had became a seething mob, might capture and do him bodily harm. There was no demonstration at this time but the next morning there was to be seen in effigy Dr. Scott's form hanging from the top of the second story of a building in course of construction on the same block. It created some excitement for the time being, but it soon simmered out.

Lloyd Tevis was getting badly frightened about this time for fear his home on the corner of Taylor and Jackson streets would be destroyed and appealed to the police for protection. He was told to go home and drape his home in black. This he did most effectually, the occasion being the assassination of President Abraham Lincoln.

One of the exciting times in San Francisco in 1865 was when a mob went to the office of "The Examiner" on Washington street near Sansome and carried everything that was movable into the street and piled it up with the intention of burning. It seems that this paper was so pronounced in its sympathy with the cause of the Confederacy that it aroused such a feeling as to cause drastic measures. The police authorities were informed of what was going on and Colonel Wood, captain of police, got a squad of policemen together and proceeded to the scene, but their movements were so slow that it was hard to tell whether they were moving or not and by the time they had reached the place the boys had carried off nearly everything that had been thrown out. I have two pieces of type now that I picked up in the street about that time.

Uncle Phil Roach, the editor, was in later years a member of the State Legislature and tried to get an appropriation to cover his loss but his efforts were of no avail.

President Lincoln and Gen. Vallejo.

President Lincoln in the early part of the Civil War called General Vallejo to Washington on business. While there General Vallejo suggested to Mr. Lincoln that the United States build a railroad into Mexico, believing as he said, it would be a benefit to both nations. Mr. Lincoln smilingly asked, "What good would it do for our people to go down to Mexico even if the railroads were built? They would all die of fever and according to your belief go down yonder," with a motion of his hand towards the supposed location of the infernal regions. "I wouldn't be very sorry about that," remarked General Vallejo coolly. "How so?" said Mr. Lincoln. "I thought you liked the Yankees." "So I do," was the answer. "The Yankees are a wonderful people, wonderful. Wherever they go they make improvements. If they were to emigrate in large numbers to hell itself, they would somehow manage to change the climate."

Off to the Nevada Mines.

Uncle Billy Rodgers, from Peoria, Ill., was a fellow passenger of mine when crossing the plains in 1849 in the first division of the "Turner, Allen & Co. Pioneer Mule Train," consisting of 40 wagons, 150 mules and 150 passengers. He was a gambler before he left home and he gambled all the way across the plains. Many people think that a gambler has no heart but this man was all heart. I knew him on one occasion, after visiting a sick man in camp, to take off his shirt and give it to the sick man and go about camp for an hour to find one for himself.

We arrived in California on September 10, 1849. We parted about that time and I saw no more of him until the winter of '68 and '69 when I was on my way to White Pine in Nevada. We had to lay over a few days at Elko, Nevada, in order to get passage in the stage. As we had saddles and bridles we made an effort to get some horses and furnish our own transportation, and we had partly made arrangements with a man by the name of Murphy. The day previous to this I overheard a conversation between two gentlemen sitting at the opposite end of a red hot stove. After they parted I approached the one left and said, "Is this Uncle Billy?" He said, "Yes, everybody calls me 'Uncle Billy' but I do not know you." I gave him my name and he was as glad to see me as I was to see him. We had a long and very pleasant chat.

Now to take up the line of march where I left off, I said, "Hold on boys a little while I go and see a friend of mine." "All right," said they. I called on Uncle Billy and told him what we were doing and asked him what kind of a man Murphy was, and his answer was,

"He's a very good blacksmith," and repeated it two or three times, then said, "I am in a wild country and never say anything against anybody." I said, "That's enough Uncle Billy, I understand you thoroughly." I parted with him and we took the stage for Hamilton and Treasure Hill. The last I heard of Uncle Billy was that he went north as an escort to some party and died there. Uncle Billy was a gambler all his life but not a drinker. His heart, his hand and his pocket were ever open and ready to respond to the relief of the distress of others. The writing of the above calls to mind another meeting with Uncle Billy of which I had lost sight, the date of which I cannot fix. I think it was in the first half of '60 I met him on the street in San Francisco and our meeting was most cordial. We had a very pleasant street visit and he said to me, "Woolley, I am going home, I shall take the next steamer for New York." I said to him, "How are you fixed, Uncle Billy?" He said, "I have eleven thousand dollars and I am going home." I congratulated him for his courage and good luck and wished him a pleasant voyage and a happy reunion with his old friends. About a week later I met Uncle Billy on the street again and said to him, "How is this Uncle Billy, I thought you were going home on the last steamer?"

"Yes," said he, "I thought so too; at the same time, I thought I would just step into a faro bank and win just enough to pay my passage home so that I would have even money when I got home. But instead of that I lost every dollar I had and I am going back into the mountains again. My readers know the rest."

My friends this is only one of thousands who had the same experience.

In 1868 "the girl I left behind me" went East on a visit of six months, taking with her our two children.

In the fall of that year (1868) I went to White Pine in Nevada. It was a very cold trip for me and I came home in June "thawed out," sold out my grocery business and went into the produce commission business and followed it for ten years.

Martin J. Burke.

Chief of Police Martin J. Burke I knew very well in the early sixties. He was a genial and good natured man, well liked by everybody who knew him. I went to him one time with a curb bit for a bridle which would bring the curb rein into action with only one pair of reins. He was much pleased with it and used one for a long while. George C. Shreve, the jeweler, had one also, as did Charles Kohler, of the firm of Kohler & Frohling, wine men of San Francisco. He offered me $3000 for my right but I refused it. I applied for a patent only to find that another was about twenty years ahead of me.

The Donahue Brothers.

James, Peter and Michael Donahue, the founders of the Union Iron Works on First and Mission streets, were three honorable, upright and just men. Their works have since been removed to the Potrero south of the Third and Townsend streets depot of the Southern Pacific Co., and have of late passed into the hands of the United Steel Corporation. They are the largest of their kind on the Pacific Coast and stand a monument to their founders. James Dunahue built and owned the Occidental Hotel on Montgomery street between Sutter and Bush streets. Peter Donahue had the foundry and machine shop. At one time there was a little misunderstanding understanding between the two and they did not speak to each other for quite a while. During this time Peter started to build an addition of brick on the north side of the foundry, got up one story and stopped. The two brothers met one day opposite the unfinished building and James said, "Peter why don't you go on and finish your building?" Peter replied, "I have not got money enough." "Oh!" said James, "go ahead and finish it up and I will let you have all the money you want." 'From that time on they resumed their brotherly relations. Peter went on in his business. His last venture was to build the Petaluma railroad. Both are now dead. Michael went East early in the '50s and I knew very little of him.

The Take of A Young Bull.

In 1870 I was in the produce commission business in San Francisco and had a consignor in Vacaville by the name of G. N. Platt who had been presented with a fine young bull by Frank M. Pixley, who lived in Sausalito, in the hills about two miles from town. Mr. Platt requested me to go and get the bull and ship him to Vacaville, so I left next morning for Sausalito. Here I sought a man who could throw the lasso. After two hours I found the man I wanted. He had the mustangs and all the necessary equipment. We mounted and left for Mr. Pixley's residence where we were informed that the animal we wanted was somewhere in the hills with the other cattle. This was rather indefinite information, but we had to make the best of it and started out. Our mustangs were well calculated for the occasion and we went over the hills like kites. Finally we saw some cattle about a mile away and we made for them, found what we were in search of and made for him. He had horns about two inches long and was as light on his feet as a deer, and gave us a lively chase for about one hour. When we had him at the end of a rope he was determined to go just the opposite way than we wanted him to, but the man and the mustang at the other end of the rope had their way part of the time, so after about two hours hard fighting we succeeded in getting the little fellow down to the wharf where I found that there would not be another boat until after dark, so I concluded to wait and come over in the morning and ship him. The next thing was to dispose of the bull for the night. I said, "Here is a coal bunker, we will put him in here." So after getting permission we started for it with the bull at one end of the rope and the vaquero at the other. The bull got a little the better of the man and went up the wharf full tilt with the vaquero in tow. The vaquero said, "There is a post on the wharf, the bull will go one side and I will go the other and round him up." But he got rounded up himself and left sprawled out on the wharf. This let the curtain down for the night and the bull went back to the hills with the rope. I returned to San Francisco, went back in the morning, hunted up my man and mustangs, mounted and went into the hills again for my bull. This was a bully ride, I enjoyed it hugely, found our game about noon, picked up the rope with the bull on the end of it. He was still wild and full of resistance. He was the hardest fellow of his size that I ever attempted to handle. We made our way back to the landing, found the boat waiting. I called the boat hands to help put him on board. They came. I put one at his head, one on each side and one behind, and they all had as much as they wanted to keep control of him. Finally he was made fast on the boat. While on our way to San Francisco a lady from the upper deck called down to me, saying, "I will give you one hundred dollars for that bull." I said, "No, madam, you cannot have him, he is going into the country for business."

After landing in San Francisco I had to take him from one wharf to another so as to take the Vacaville boat. I got a job wagon and the boat hands to take him out and tie the fellow to the hind axle of the wagon and then go by his side to the other boat. We fastened him securely to a stanchion and tagged to his destination. This relieved me of any further responsibility. I saw him about three years later in Vacaville. He was a fine large fellow with all the fire in his eye that he had in his younger days. He had a large ring in his nose with a chain running from it to the end of each horn. Now as my readers have had the bear story, and now the bull story, they will excuse me on those two subjects.

Admission Day 1875.

Another event that might be of interest and worthy of reciting here on account of the many noted personages that partook in the celebration was the ceremonies connected with the 25th anniversary of the admission of California as a State into the Union, September 9, 1875.

The principal places of business, banks and offices were all closed and the buildings and streets were gaily bedecked with flags and bunting. The "bear flag" being in evidence everywhere. The shipping presented a pretty sight, the vessels seeming to outvie each other in their efforts to display the greatest amount of bunting and flags.

One of the features of the day was the parade. The procession started from in front of the Hall of the Pioneers on Montgomery street north of Jackson, marched along Montgomery to Market, to

Eleventh, to Mission and thence to Woodward's Gardens, where the exercises were held. When opposite the Lick House, James Lick, the honored president of the society, who reviewed the passing pioneers from his rooms, was given a rousing salute by each of the delegations as they passed. In this parade were members of the pioneer organizations from Sacramento, Stockton, Marysville, Vallejo, Sonoma, Marin, Napa, Mendocino, Lake and Placerville, as well as the parent organization of San Francisco.

The escort consisted of the 1st, 2nd and 3rd Regiments, 2nd Brigade, N. G. C., Col. W. H. L. Barnes, Col. John McComb and Col. Archie Wason, respectively. Brig. Gen. John Hewston, Jr., commanding. Marshal Huefner and his aide followed. Next came the several visiting pioneer organizations, then the carriages of invited guests, orator, reader and others. Then the home society, turning out 427 strong.

Among the persons of note to have been seen and who wore the golden badge indicating that they had come here prior to 1849, were Carlos F. Glein, A. A. Green, A. G. Abel, George Graft, W. P. Toler, Thos. Edgar, G. W. Ross, P. Kadel, F. Ballhaus, W. C. Hinckley, H. B. Russ, A. G. Russ, Owen Murry, B. P. Kooser, J. E. Winson, Arthur Cornwall, E. A. Engleberg, Wm. Jeffry, Capt. Hinckley, Wm. Huefner, Thos. Roche, F. G. Blume, John C. Ball and Thomas Eagar.

Among the others present were Ex-Gox. Low, Mayor Otis, Ex-Sen. Cole, Chas. Clayton, Paul K. Hubbs of Vallejo, Eleazer Frisbie, L. B. Mizner, Niles Searles, F. W. McKinstry and Dr. O. M. Wozencraft, a member of the First Constitutional Convention of California.

In the Sonoma delegation were Nicholas Carriger, ex-president and director; Wm. Hargrave, a member of the original Bear Flag Party of 1846, Mrs. W. M. Boggs and Mrs. A. J. Grayson, who came here in 1846 in advance of the Donner party.

In the Vallejo delegation were John Paul Jones Donaldson, then 84 years old, who was on this coast as early as 1823 and who came back to reside here in 1848.

Wm. Boggs and his delegation from Sonoma were mostly all 1846 arrivals.

James W. Marshall, the man who discovered gold at Coloma, about 45 miles northeast from Sacramento, on January 19th, 1848, was with the Sacramento delegation. He was then 67 years old, hale and hearty.

Mr. Murphy, a survivor of the Donner party, was with the Marysville delegation.

In addition to these were many others who have since become well known through their doings in the political arena and business world, and have made names for themselves that are honored and respected to this day and will ever find a place in this State's history.

At the Pavilion in Woodward's Gardens the literary services were held. D. J. Staples, acting-president, delivered a stirring address, rehearsing the events of the past 25 years.

Dr. J. B. Stillman then followed with an oration in which he spoke of the gold discovery in California, the effect upon the East of Col. Mason's report, the sudden influx of seekers of the "Golden Fleece" by sea and overland, of their hardships and endurance, and their experiences at the mines, etc., etc.

Mr. J. B. Benton read a poem by Mrs. James Neall.

The literary exercises were followed by a lunch and that by an entertainment of mixed character. Billy Emerson, Ben Cotton, Billy Rice, Ernest Linden, F. Oberist, W. F. Baker, J. G. Russell and Billy Arlington of Maguire's Minstrel Troupe, and W. S. Lawton, Capt. Martin and L. P. Ward, and the Buisley family being among the entertainers.

A balloon ascension followed the entertainment and during the day the "Great Republic" made an excursion around the bay.

On an S. P. Pay-Car.

In the summer of 1874 the paymaster of the Southern Pacific Railroad Company, Major J. M. Hanford, sent me an invitation to accompany him on the pay car through the San Joaquin Valley, to pay off the employees of the company. I was delighted to have an opportunity of going through the valley. At the appointed time I was on hand with two boxes of cigars, for I knew the Major was likely to have some lively, good natured fellows with him, and I wanted to have something with me to help me along. Now I must say something about this pay car, for it was a wonderful thing for me. It had the appearance on the inside of a hotel on wheels. At the rear end was a window through which the employees were paid; the depth of the room in which were the pay master and his two check clerks, was about the same as the width of the car. In it were the safe, rifles, shotguns, pistols, ammunition galore, with an opening into what was used as the dining room and berths, which would accommodate about 12 people. Then came the cook's room on one side, with a narrow passageway on the other, into a small room in the front end of the car. This car was sixty feet in length and would make you think you were in a palace hotel on wheels. Hank Small, who had hands as big as a garden spade, was the engineer, with engine No. 96, which was always expected to pull the pay car. Then there was a man by the name of Olmsby who was one of the check clerks, young and very fine looking. Then there was another man in the employ of the company by the name of Gerald who was auditor for the company and had feet twice as large as any other man. Now I want my readers to hold these three men in mind and their peculiarities for I shall refer to them later on.

We are all now seated at the supper table, ten in all, and all railroad men except myself, with the dignified paymaster at the head of the table and his check clerk, Olmsby, at the foot, who assumed the duty of saying grace by making motions around his chest and head, accompanied with these words, "Bucksaws filed and set." This created some amusement and was the only time it occurred. The supper went on and the tables were cleared away, and then there was chatting and story telling. Finally I started to tell a story and had gotten fairly into it when I suddenly discovered that every man in the room was sound asleep. It did not take me long to wake them up and have every man on his feet or on the floor. This did not last long, for I brought out one of my boxes of cigars and that settled the question right there. The next day we were in the San Joaquin Valley and continued the trip, paying the men as we went along, until we reached Bakersfield. This was the end of the road at that time.

Then we returned to Stockton, to Sacramento, to Red Bluff, which was the end of the road in that direction at that time. From there we returned to San Francisco, having had a very fine and agreeable trip, and each one returned to his former allotted position. I at this time was in the produce commission business on Washington street near Front street. Inside of a year Mr. Olmsby left the railroad company, married and went to Chico, in the Sacramento Valley, to run a stationery store. In 1876, the year that President Hayes was elected, his wife gave birth to a child and Olmsby sent a telegram to Mr. Hanford reading like this: "Boy, born last night, has Gerald's feet, Hank Small's hands, my good looks, and hollered for Hayes all night."

Employ of the Southern Pacific.

In 1884 I went into the employ of the Southern Pacific Co. where I remained for twenty years. In 1904 on account of a rule of the company pertaining to long service and age, I was retired on a pension. I protested, they insisted, I accepted (because I could not help myself). The company was right and I appreciated the pension as they appreciated my services. In all those years I had no reason to complain of the company.

Shortly after my retirement from the employ of the Southern Pacific Company I had sickness in my family and lost "the girl I left behind me," after fifty-three years of happy married life. This was in 1906, it is now 1913, and I am still behind, but I shall get there bye-and-bye and we will go on together side by side.

Sloat Monument.

On June 4, 1910, I went to Monterey, Calif., to attend the ceremonies of the unveiling and dedication of the Sloat Monument at the Presidio of Monterey. The idea, conception and putting through to a successful termination of the erection of this monument, was the work of, we might say, one man, Major Edwin A. Sherman, V. M. W. It has taken the greater part of his time for twenty-four years. A large proportion of the money necessary was raised by subscription, but things lagged for a while, when the Major applied to the U. S. Congress for an appropriation of $10,000 to complete the work and got it. The monument was then finished under the supervision of Lieutenant-Colonel John Biddle.

At the dedication which was held under the auspices of the Grand Lodge of Masons, Col. C. W. Mason, U. S. A., delivered the address of welcome, Major Sherman gave a brief sketch of the work and Lt.-Col. Biddle made a few remarks. M. W. W. Frank Pierce, 33rd degree Mason, officiated.

The monument was erected to commemorate the raising of the American Flag at Monterey, the capital of California, July 7, 1846, by the forces under command of Com. Jonathan Drake Sloat, U. S. N. War had been declared between the U. S. and Mexico.

Nob Hill.

In later days, about 1877, the term Nob Hill was applied to the crown of California street from Powell street westward three blocks to Jones street, on account of its having been selected by the railroad magnates of the State upon which to build their new homes, it being their desire to live together in their home life as well as in their business life.

On the north side of California street commencing at Powell was the residence of Mr. David Porter. This was torn down to make way for the Fairmont Hotel, ground for which was broken October 15, 1902. There were other small homes on other parts of the block but they too were removed and the entire block was used as a site for this famous hostelry.

In the early days a long shanty 40 feet by 10 to 12 feet in width stood where the Porter residence formerly stood. A man by the name of McIntire owned it. It was literally covered with California honeysuckle, and a view point of the town. This entire block was acquired by the late James G. Fair, one of the famous mining men of Nevada, and it still remains in the family estate. The hotel was in the course of construction at the time of the great fire of April 18-21,

1906, and the interior had to be rebuilt entirely as well as the stonework about the exterior openings.

The next of the large homes was that of James C. Flood, a handsome and imposing structure of Connecticut brownstone. This building stood upon the eastern half of the block between Mason and Taylor streets and in order to build, a huge hill of rock as high as the building now is, had to be removed. This was in 1876. After the fire of 1906 this building was remodeled and is now occupied by the Pacific-Union Club.

Mason street had just been cut through this same hill. On the west half of the block stood the home of the late D. D. Colton, who made his fortune out of construction contracts on the Central Pacific railroad. It was afterwards purchased by C. P. Huntington, another of the famous railroad magnates.

On the next corner stood the large frame mansion of Charles Crocker, one of the builders of the C. P. R. R., built at an expense of $2,500,000. His son William H. built himself a home on the far corner of the same block. This takes us to Jones street. When the late Charles Crocker selected this site for his home there was one piece of property facing on Sacramento street that he could not buy, so in order to get even with the owner, a Mr. Young, he had a tall spite fence built around the house. The owner lived there for a while, but being shut off as he was from the sunlight, had his house removed; still he would not sell and the fence stood there for years afterwards.

On the south side of the street commencing at Powell stood the mansion of Ex-Governor Leland Stanford. When Stanford purchased the property there stood there a fine house built by the actress Julia Dean Hayne, with an entrance at the corner. This house was removed to the corner of Pine and Hyde streets.

The stone retaining wall on Powell and Pine streets, owing to a spring on the property, gave way and had to be taken down (at the corner) and rebuilt. At the corner it extends 20 feet below the sidewalk and is 20 feet thick and 30 feet high. The ground was then terraced.

The building cost in the neighborhood of $2,000,000.

On the corner above, Mark Hopkins built his home. At his death it passed into the hands of a Mr. Searles who had married Hopkins' widow and, not caring to live in California, he had it converted into an art gallery, and the beautiful conservatory into art rooms for the Art Association of the University of California, to whom he bequeathed the property. The building cost in the neighborhood Of $2,750,000.

On the next block, between Mason and Taylor streets, were the Hamilton home, the home of Ex-Mayor E. B. Pond and that of the Tobins. While on the block from Taylor to Jones street stood the A. N. Towne, H. H. Sherwood and George Whittell residences. Just beyond Jones street, on the same side, stood the home of E. J. (Lucky) Baldwin of race horse fame.

In 1861 I moved to 1211 Taylor street, between Clay and Washington, and resided there continuously until 1878, a period of 17 years. And I knew of Stanford, Hopkins, Crocker and Huntington, the quartet of railroad magnates, better than they knew of me. But what shall I say of them? They have all gone beyond the boundaries of human existence and their mansions, together with all the other homes on the hill, were burned in the fire of April 18-21, 1906. They were all men of master minds and are deserving the highest praise for their enterprise, determination and perseverance in the great work they undertook. It was not their money that did it, it was their heads. And there is where the great indebtedness of the State of California comes in to these men.

Going down the eastern slope on California, just below Powell on the south side, at the corner of Prospect Place, stood a house once occupied by Lieut. John Charles Fremont, while on the corner below stood the home of Col. Jonathan D. Stevenson. This building was built in 1851 and had two tiers of verandas that extended entirely around the building. The Colonel died at the age of 94 but had not owned or lived there for many years. It had been converted into a hotel and known as the Harvey House.

Across the street on the other corner stood the Grace Episcopal Church. The Crocker heirs, not desiring to rebuild on their property on California, between Taylor and Jones streets, bequeathed it to the

Episcopal Diocese on which to build a new Grace Church. It is now in course of construction.

On Pine street, at the southwest corner of Stockton, stood the Wilson home. On the southeast corner of Mason stood the home of J. D. Oliver, while on the southwest corner stood the home of Mr. Fred McCrellish, the owner of the "Alta California," while just beyond were the homes of Woods, Jarboe and Harrison and others. On the next block was the old Stow residence while across the street Isaiah W. Lees, chief of police, resided. He was the greatest detective this coast has ever had—his was instinct and intuition, and his records will always remain a lasting monument. On the northwest corner of Jones stood the home of the late James G. Fair, of mining fame, of Nevada.

Going north on Powell street, at No. 812, Mr. Chilion Beach, the bookseller, lived, while next door, No. 814, Mr. D. D. Shattuck resided. This building was erected in 1854—Mr. Shattuck came to California via the Isthmus and resided here 47 years. On the next block (same side) stood a little one-story house with a high basement in which J. D. Spencer, a brother of Spencer the sociologist, lived for many years. Just beyond stood the old High School building. On the next block, at No. 1010, resided for many years another of the old booksellers, Mr. George B. Hitchcock, proprietor of the "Pioneer Book Store," opposite the "Plaza."

At the northwest corner of Washington stood the first brick building built in San Francisco. It was built in 1851 by John Truebody, the brick being brought from New York. It was originally two stories high but upon the grading of the streets it was built another story downward to the new grade. He later added another story, the fourth, on top. Even to the time of the fire (1906) you could see the various stairway landings on the Washington street frontage. Mr. Truebody originally owned this entire block.

The first church building in Yerba Buena (as San Francisco was formerly called) was the First Presbyterian Church on the west side of Powell near Washington. It was built in 1849 of hand-hewn timbers from Oregon. Upon the erection of the First Methodist Church it was moved to the rear and used as a Sunday school. John Truebody constructed it.

In this immediate neighborhood were many a frame building that had been brought around the Horn "in the knocked down state."

Powell street, from Clay to North Beach, was graded in 1854. It and Stockton street to the east, from Sacramento street north to Green street, were lined with neat homes and was then considered the fashionable residence section of the city, while on Powell street were three churches.

The streets in those days were all planked. Beyond Mason streets ran the trail westward to the Presidio, past scattered cottages, sheds, dairies and vegetable gardens.

On the east side of Stockton street, between Sacramento and Clay streets, stood the old Pioche residence, wherein were given many lavish entertainments, for its owner was an epicure and hospitable to a degree. He was a heavy speculator and at one time possessed of much property. His death was a mystery and has never been solved. During the '90's his home was used as the Chinese consulate.

On the west side of Taylor street at the corner of Sacramento street stood the home of Capt. J. B. Thomas, after occupied by Addison E. Head, while on the corner of Clay I had my grocery business, living on the next block, between Clay and Washington, No. 1211. Win. T. Coleman, the leader of the Vigilance Committee, lived on the corner of Washington street; this house was built by W. F. Walton, and occupied in turn by S. C. Hastings, Wm. T. Coleman and D. M. Delmas, all men of prominence, while on the next corner stood the home of my old friend, Gross, who came across the plains with me in 1849. In later days, Mr. Chilion Beach resided there.

On the east side at the southeast corner of Washington, stood the J. B. Haggin home, while on the northeast corner stood that of the Beavers, and at the corner of Jackson, the Tevis.' In this neighborhood also lived Ina D. Coolbrith, whose home was the center of the literary genius of the State, amongst them being Bret Harte, Joaquin Miller, and Charles Warren Stoddard. Josiah Stanford, a brother of Leland Stanford, lived on the south side of Jackson street, just below the Tevis home.

Here is as good a place as any to give my readers a short account of the Clay Street Hill Underground Cable Railroad, which operated on Clay street from Leavenworth to Kearny streets, a distance of seven blocks, and at an elevation of 307 feet above the starting point. The cable car was the invention of Mr. A. S. Hallidie, who organized the company which built the line. This was the first time that the application of an underground cable was ever used to move street cars, and on August 1, 1873, the first run up the Clay street hill from Kearny to Leavenworth street, was made, and by September 1st the road was in operation. It was a wonderful exhibition, and half the town was there to witness it. Many were in doubt as to the success of the enterprise. The company required the property holders on the hill to subscribe and donate towards the expense, which they did. The writer owning some property there at that time, gave $100.00 to further the enterprise. This was in 1872. An interested Chinese watched the moving cars and remarked: "No pushee, no pullee, go like hellee."

The California Street Railroad Company used the same device. This line was operated along California street from Kearny to Fillmore and first operated April 9, 1878. It was afterwards extended eastward to Drumm and Market streets and westward to Central Avenue. The Sutter Street R. R. Co. was in operation January 27, 1877, and the Geary street line, February 16, 1880. Cable cars were also operated over Sacramento and Washington streets as well as over Powell at later dates.

[1] A few words might be said concerning the principals of this trouble. King, whose name was James King (before coming to California he had added "of William" so as to distinguish himself from others of that name), came to California November 10th, 1848, engaged in mining and mercantile pursuits and in December 1849 engaged in the banking business in San Francisco. In 1854 he merged with Adams & Co. Shortly afterwards they failed, and he lost everything he possessed. Through the financial backing of his friends, he started the "Daily Evening Bulletin," October 8th, 1855, a small four-page sheet about 10 x 15 inches in size. He was fearless in his editorials, but always within the bounds of right and justice, and

took a strong position against corruption of the city officials and their means of election. His paper grew in circulation and size, and soon outstripped all the other papers combined. November 17th, 1855, the Cora and Richardson affair held the attention of the public, and King in his fearlessness inflamed the population into taking matters into their own hands after the Courts had failed to convict. And by his so doing had aroused an enmity, and determination from the lawless element to stop his utterances, even at the cost of his life, so when he attacked in his paper, one James P. Casey, a lawless character, gambler and ballot box manipulator and Supervisor, as having served an eighteen-months sentence in Sing Sing, N. Y., before coming to California, who also published a paper, "The Sunday Times," it brought matters to a crisis, for Casey taking offense at this and other attacks on his ilk, shot King on the evening of May 14, 1856. The shooting of King was the cause of the formation of the Vigilance Committee of 1856 and the direct means of cleaning the city of the corruptness that had had swing for so many years.—[Editor.]

[2] Two of the unused cartridges of Mr. Woolley's, at the end of the troublous time of the Vigilance committee, are to be seen in the Oakland Public Museum.—[Editor.]

[3] A large number of the citizens of San Francisco interested themselves toward caring and providing for the family of the deceased, Mr. King, and through the efforts of Mr. F. W. Macondray and six others, collected nearly $36,000. They had erected a monument in Lone Mountain Cemetery, supported the family, and in 1868 the money which, had by judicious investment amounted to nearly $40,000, about half of this fund, was turned over to the elder children, leaving $22,000 on deposit, but this, through the bank's failure, netted the family only $15,000.

[4] The body of James King, of William, was buried In Lone Mountain Cemetery, that of James P. Casey in Mission Dolores Cemetery, by the members of Crescent Engine Company No. 10, of which he was foreman, while that of Charles Cora was delivered to Belle Cora and its final resting place is unknown to this day, though it has been stated that she had it buried in Mission Dolores Cemetery.—[Editor.]

[5] His body was interred in Mission Dolores Cemetery.—[Editor.]

[6] The name of this "Betsy Ross" has been lost, though Mr. Connell probably knew it at the time. The flag, except for the blue field, is badly faded.—[Editor.]